Advent
with
Evelyn Underhill

Advent
with
Evelyn Underhill

edited by
Christopher L. Webber

MOREHOUSE PUBLISHING
HARRISBURG—NEW YORK

Morehouse Publishing, P.O. Box 1321, Harrisburg, PA 17105

Morehouse Publishing, 445 Fifth Avenue, New York, NY 10016

Morehouse Publishing is an imprint of Church Publishing Incorporated.

Cover art: *The Literature Window* (Christ Church, Bronxville, New York). The artist, Ellen Miret-Jayson, has begun this set of three windows with a center lancet that sums up the mystical journey as described by Underhill. The bottom panel begins with organic forms floating and rising to form a more cohesive unit (the ability to meditate), which is surrounded by black since the first stage of the journey involves purgation, simplification, and cleansing. As the soul continues to rise, she writes, it becomes more unified and is surrounded by white, the illuminative phase. A blazing star at this level symbolizes the mystic's quest. The soul rises further for the ultimate union with the Absolute, and here it is surrounded by red, or the fire of the Spirit. The light of the Spirit reaches through all levels. The goal of the quest, Jerusalem, has been reached.

The lancet to the left is based on words in Donne's "Holy Sonnet IV."
    But who shall give thee that grace to begin?

The center lancet is based on a phrase from Underhill's *Mysticism*.
    . . . only the Real can know Reality.

The lancet to the right begins with a quotation from T. S. Eliot's Quartet, "Burnt Norton."
    I can only say, *there* we have been: but I cannot say where.

Cover design: Laurie Westhafer

Library of Congress Cataloging-in-Publication Data

Underhill, Evelyn, 1875–1941.
  Advent with Evelyn Underhill / edited by Christopher L. Webber.
    p. cm.
  Includes index.
  ISBN-13: 978-0-8192-2221-3 (pbk.)
  1. Advent—Meditations. 2. Christmas—Meditations. I. Webber, Christopher.
II. Title.
  BV40.U53 2006
  242'.33—dc22
                                    2006018138

Printed in the United States of America

06 07 08 09   10 9 8 7 6 5 4 3 2 1

Introduction

Evelyn Underhill was born in Wolverhampton, England, on December 6, 1875, the only child of Arthur Underhill, a barrister, and his wife, Alice Lucy, whose father was a justice of the peace in Wolverhampton. Evelyn was educated primarily at home, but spent three years at a private school in Folkestone before studying history and botany at King's College for Women in London. In 1907 she married Hubert Stuart Moore, a barrister, whom she had known since childhood.

Although she had once considered herself an atheist, she became increasingly interested in the life of the spirit and wrote major studies on mysticism and worship. As her understanding of the Christian faith developed, Underhill was torn between the Roman and Anglican traditions. She eventually settled into the Anglican way because, as Dana Greene, president of the Evelyn Underhill Association, has written, she thought that "the demands of Rome postulated a surrender of her intellectual honor."

"Spirituality" has become a far more familiar term in early-twenty-first-century society than it was in the first part of the twentieth century when Evelyn Underhill wrote and taught. She was a pioneer, one might say, of the current revival of interest in spiritual growth. But unlike so much of the wide range of thought and practice now included under the broad term "spirituality," Evelyn Underhill's work was solidly grounded in the great tradition of Christian spirituality. Underhill said that "the spiritual life is a dangerously ambiguous term" and suggested that for all too many it means "the life of my own inside." For Underhill, spirituality was about reality and a God who came into the real world to meet and transform real people. Prayer, sacraments, and life within the church were central to her teaching and practice. She drew freely from the medieval mystics, the Orthodox tradition, and the insights of contemporary psychiatry, but she could illustrate her teaching with references to gardening, music, and mountain climbing. God, she believed, came into and was present in all of life.

As she grew older, Underhill gave more and more of her time to spiritual guidance for individuals and retreat groups. Many of her later books are transcripts of talks given at retreats to groups seeking God's presence in their lives. This emphasis on God's presence in all life, especially the incarnation of God in Jesus Christ, makes Underhill an ideal guide to the keeping of Advent. The four weeks before Christmas are a season dedicated to preparation for Christ's coming. We remember how he came once and we pray that he may come again to us and our world. This is a constant theme in Underhill's meditations.

In selecting brief paragraphs from Underhill's writing for Advent meditations, it seemed best to keep the emphasis on a few central themes. After two opening meditations tied closely to the meaning of Advent, there is a sequence on various aspects of the spiritual life: discipline, humility, patience, maturity, and others. Moving closer to Christmas, there is a series of meditations on prayer, and then, just before Christmas, love becomes the focus because it is love that comes to us in the incarnate Christ. The fourteen days of Christmas begin with meditations on the meaning of incarnation, always a central theme for Underhill; the attention then shifts to the Magi whose coming is celebrated at the end of the Christmas season.

Those using this book should note that, since the Advent season can vary in length, meditations have been provided for the longest Advent possible. The meditations are dated to begin on November 27 whether Advent does so in a particular year or not. To help readers make the fullest use of the readings, a brief thought for meditation has been provided for each day as well as a prayer based on the reading.

Advent
with
Evelyn Underhill

NOVEMBER 27

Recognition and Expectancy

At the beginning of her course the Church looks out towards Eternity, and realizes her own poverty and imperfection and her utter dependence on this perpetual coming of God. Advent is, of course, first of all a preparation for Christmas; which commemorates God's saving entrance into history in the Incarnation of Jesus Christ.

Whilst all things were in quiet silence and night was in the midst of her swift course:

thine Almighty Word leapt down from heaven out of thy royal throne. Alleluia.

A tremendous spiritual event then took place; something which disclosed the very nature of God and His relation to His universe. But there was little to show for it on the surface of life. All men saw was a poor girl unconditionally submitted to God's Will, and a baby born in difficult circumstances. And this contrast between the outward appearance and the inner reality is true of all the coming of God to us. We must be very loving and very alert if we want to recognise them in their earthly disguise. Again and again He comes and the revelation is not a bit what we expect.

So the next lesson Advent should teach us is that our attitude towards Him should always be one of humble eager expectancy. Our spiritual life depends on His perpetual coming to us, far more than on our going to Him. Every time a channel is made for Him He comes; every time our hearts are open to Him He enters, bringing a fresh gift of His very life, and on that life we depend. We should think of the whole power and splendour of God as always pressing in upon our small souls. "In Him we live and move and have our being."

For meditation: Whenever our hearts are open to Him He enters.

For prayer: Even so, come, Lord Jesus, and let our hearts be open to receive the life that you alone can give.

NOVEMBER 28

A Sense of Need

We should think of the whole power and splendour of God as always pressing in upon our small souls. "In Him we live and move and have our being." But that power and splendour mostly reach us in homely and inconspicuous ways; in the sacraments, and in our prayers, joys and sorrows and in all opportunities of loving service. This means that one of the most important things in our prayer is the eagerness and confidence with which we throw ourselves open to His perpetual coming. There should always be more waiting than striving in a Christian's prayer—an absolute dependence on the self-giving charity of God. "As dew shall our God descend on us."

As we draw near Christmas, this sense of our own need and of the whole world's need of God's coming—never greater perhaps than it is now—becomes more intense. In the great Advent Antiphons which are said in the week before Christmas we seem to hear the voice of the whole suffering creation saying "Come! give us wisdom, give us light, deliver us, liberate us, lead us, teach us how to live. Save us." And we, joining in that prayer, unite our need with the one need of the whole world. We have to remember that the answer to the prayer was not a new and wonderful world order but Bethlehem and the Cross; a life of complete surrender to God's Will; and we must expect this answer to be worked out in our own lives in terms of humility and sacrifice.

If our lives are ruled by this spirit of Advent, this loving expectation of God, they will have a quality quite different from that of conventional piety. For they will be centred on an entire and conscious dependence upon the supernatural love which supports us; hence all self-confidence will be destroyed in them and replaced by perfect confidence in God. They will be docile to His pressure, and obedient to every indication of His Will.

For meditation: All self-confidence [must be] replaced by perfect confidence in God.

For prayer: Come! Give us wisdom, give us light, deliver us, liberate us, lead us, teach us how to live. Save us.

November 29

Starting Out

Everyone who is engaged on a great undertaking, depending on many factors for its success, knows how important it is to have a periodical stocktaking. Whether we are responsible for a business, an institution, a voyage, or an exploration—even for the well-being of a household—it is sometimes essential to call a halt; examine our stores and our equipment, be sure that all necessaries are there and in good order, and that we understand the way in which they should be used. It is no good to have tins without tin openers, bottles of which the contents have evaporated, labels written in an unknown language, or mysterious packages of which we do not know the use.

Now the living-out of the spiritual life, the inner life of the Christian—the secret correspondence of his soul with God—is from one point of view a great business. It was well called "the business of all businesses" by St. Bernard; for it is no mere addition to Christianity, but its very essence, the source of its vitality and power. From another point of view it is a great journey; a bit-by-bit progress, over roads that are often difficult and in weather that is sometimes pretty bad, from "this world to that which is to come." Whichever way we look at it, an intelligent and respectful attitude to our equipment—seeing that it is all there, accessible and in good condition, and making sure that we know the real use of each item—is essential to success. It is only too easy to be deluded by the modern craving for peace and immediate results, and press on without pausing to examine the quality and character of our supplies, or being sure that we know where we are going and possess the necessary maps. But this means all the disabling miseries of the unmarked route and unbalanced diet, and at last, perhaps, complete loss of bearings and consequent starvation of the soul.

For meditation: [Be] sure that we know where we are going.

For prayer: Make us, Lord God, deeply aware of the task before us and our need for guidance on the way.

NOVEMBER 30

Spiritual Life: Begin with Objective Fact

The spiritual life is a stern choice. It is not a consoling retreat from the difficulties of existence; but an invitation to enter fully into that difficult existence, and there apply the Charity of God and bear the cost. Till we accept this truth, religion is full of puzzles for us, and its practices often unmeaning: for we do not know what it is all about. So there are few things more bracing and enlightening than a deliberate resort to [some basic] statements about God, the world and the soul; testing by them our attitude to those realities, and the quality and vigour of our interior life with God. For every one of them has a direct bearing on that interior life. *Lex credendi, lex orandi.* Our prayer and belief should fit like hand and glove; they are the inside and outside of one single correspondence with God.

Since the life of prayer consists in an ever-deepening communion with a Reality beyond ourselves, which is truly there, and touches, calls, attracts us, what we believe about that Reality will rule our relation to it. We do not approach a friend and a machine in the same way. We make the first and greatest of our mistakes in religion when we begin with ourselves, our petty feelings and needs, ideas and capacities. The Creed sweeps us up past all this to God, the objective Fact, and His mysterious self-giving to us. It sets first Eternity and then History before us, as the things that truly matter in religion; and shows us a humble and adoring delight in God as the first duty of the believing soul. So there can hardly be a better inward discipline than the deliberate testing of our vague, dilute, self-occupied spirituality by this superb vision of Reality.

For meditation: Delight in God [is] the first duty of the believing soul.

For prayer: Open our eyes, Lord God, to the reality of your presence in our world and our lives.

December 1

Shut the Door

Now Christ, who so seldom gave detailed instruction about anything, did give some detailed instruction for that withdrawal, that recollection which is the essential condition of real prayer, real communion with God.

"Thou when thou prayest, enter into thy closet—and *shut the door.*"

I think we can almost see the smile with which He said those three words: and those three words define what we have to try to do. Anyone can retire into a quiet place and have a thoroughly unquiet time in it—but that is not making a Retreat! It is the shutting of the door which makes the whole difference between a true Retreat and a worried religious weekend.

Shut the door. It is an extraordinary difficult thing to do. Nearly every one pulls it to and leaves it slightly ajar so that a whistling draught comes in from the outer world, with reminders of all the worries, interests, conflicts, joys and sorrows of daily life.

But Christ said Shut, and He meant Shut. A complete barrier deliberately set up, with you on one side alone with God and everything else without exception on the other side. The voice of God is very gentle; we cannot hear it if we let other voices compete. Our ordinary life, of course, is not lived like that and should not be; but this bit of life is to be lived like that. It is no use at all to enter that closet, that inner sanctuary, clutching the daily paper, the reports of all the societies you support, your engagement book and a large bundle of personal correspondence. All these must be left outside. The motto . . . is *God Only*, God in Himself, sought for Himself alone.

The object . . . is not Intercession or self exploration, but such communion with Him as shall afterwards make you more powerful in intercession; and such self-loss in Him as shall heal your wounds by new contact with His life and love.

For meditation: We cannot hear [God's voice] if we let other voices compete.

For prayer: Grant me a spirit of silence, Holy God, and an ability to shut out competing voices so that I hear your voice clearly and your voice alone.

December 2

Patience

Christ never seems at first sight to be giving pure truth; yet in the end He is the only teacher who manages to give it in a way that feeds souls of every level and type. Wherever He comes, He brings the life-giving mystery of God: but giving the mystery in and with the homeliness, weaving together both worlds.

What a lesson for us! And especially for those who have a secret arrogant craving for what they call "purely spiritual things." There is nothing abstract or high-brow about Him. To all He gives parables capable of simple interpretation and to some revelations within them of the Mysteries of the Kingdom of Heaven. There is no overfeeding or straining of souls and, above all, no hurry to enlighten at all costs everyone He can reach. What a great supernatural art that is—that quiet, humble patience; whether of those who teach or of those being taught. Whichever class we think we are in, we are all studying under the quiet eye of God; and we have got to learn the artist's pace, never to hurry or scramble or lose our breath, yet never to wait too long; to put on a good primary coat and *let it dry* in spite of our eagerness to get on with the picture before the inspiration fades; the only result of which is a sticky mess.

Christ seems so often content to prepare souls by one great revealing truth and then just leave grace to act, to fertilize, to bring forth, to give light with that easy generosity and not ask about results. To leave it to God, to make no effort to harvest one's own corn and say, "See

11

what a lot of sheaves *I* have brought in!"—that asks for a self-oblivion which is very near the Cross.

For meditation: We have to learn the artist's pace.

For prayer: Let me be content, Lord Jesus, to allow your grace to work in me calmly and quietly and at a pace that seems good to you.

DECEMBER 3

Humility

Humility and moderation at the heart of our prayer quiet the soul and protect us against the spiritual itch. "It sometimes comes into my head," says De Caussade, "to wonder whether I have ever properly confessed my sins, whether God has ever forgiven me my sins, whether I am in a good or bad spiritual state. What progress have I made in prayer or the interior life? When this happens I say to myself at once, God has chosen to hide all this from me, so that I may just blindly abandon myself to His mercy. So I submit myself and adore His decision. . . . He is the Master: may all that He wills be accomplished in me; I want no grace, no merit, no perfection but that which shall please Him. His will alone is sufficient for me and that will always be the measure of my desires." Meekness and temperance taught out of his own experience by a very great master of the spiritual life. In your soul's life towards God, then, that humble moderation has, or should have, an important place and many special applications. It is far better to realize a few truths, produce a few acts of worship, but do them *well*, leaving to others those truths and those practices which for you are dark or involve strain. Do not entertain the notion that you ought to advance in your prayer. If you do, you will only find out you have put on the brake instead of the accelerator. All real progress in spiritual things comes gently, imperceptibly, and is the work of God. Our crude efforts spoil it. Know yourself for the childish, limited and dependent soul you are. Remember that the only growth that matters happens without our knowledge and that trying to stretch ourselves is both dangerous and silly. Think of the Infinite Goodness, never of your own state. Realize that the very capacity to pray at all is the free gift of the divine love and be content with St. Francis de Sales' favourite prayer, in which all personal religion is summed up: "Yes, Father! Yes! and always Yes!"

For meditation: All real progress in spiritual things comes gently, imperceptibly.

For prayer: Help me to remember, Holy God, that my prayer is your gift and that I need no other prayer than the one you have given.

December 4

Discipline

All normal men and women possess, at least in a rudimentary form, some intuition of the transcendental; shown in their power of experiencing beauty or love. In some it is dominant emerging easily and without help; in others it is latent and must be developed in the right way. In others again it may exist in virtual conflict with a strongly realistic outlook; gathering way until it claims its rights at last in a psychic storm. Its emergence, however achieved, is a part—and for our true life, by far the most important part—of that outcropping and overflowing into consciousness of the marginal faculties which is now being recognized as essential to all artistic and creative activities; and as playing, too, a large part in the regulation of mental and bodily health.

All the great religions have implicitly understood—though without analysis—the vast importance of these spiritual intuitions and faculties lying below the surface of the everyday mind; and have perfected machinery tending to secure their release and their training. This is of two kinds: first, religious ceremonial, addressing itself to corporate feeling; next the discipline of meditation and prayer, which educates the individual to the same ends, gradually developing the powers of the foreconscious region, steadying them, and bringing them under the control of the purified will. Without some such education, widely as its details may vary, there can be no real living of the spiritual life.

For meditation: Without discipline there can be no real spiritual life.

For prayer: Help me, Holy God, to bring my life under your control with a plan and pattern that reminds me of your presence and makes me more responsive to your will.

DECEMBER 5

Intimations of Spiritual Depths

Many Christians are like deaf people at a concert. They study the programme carefully, believe every statement made in it, speak respectfully of the quality of the music, but only really hear a phrase now and again. So they have no notion at all of the mighty symphony which fills the universe, to which our lives are destined to make their tiny contribution, and which is the self-expression of the Eternal God.

Yet there are plenty of things in our normal experience, which imply the existence of that world, that music, that life. If, for instance, we consider the fact of prayer, the almost universal impulse to seek and appeal to a power beyond ourselves, and notice the heights to which it can rise in those who give themselves to it with courage and love—the power it exerts, the heroic vocations and costly sacrifices which it supports, the transformations of character which it effects—it is a sufficiently mysterious characteristic of man. Again and again it is discredited by our popular rationalisms and naturalisms, and again and again it returns, and claims its rights within human life; even in its crudest, most naive expressions retaining a certain life-changing power. No one who studies with sympathy, for instance, the history of religious revivals, can doubt that here, often in a grotesque and unlovely disguise, a force from beyond the world really breaks in upon the temporal order with disconcerting power.

So, too, all who are sensitive to beauty know the almost agonising sense of revelation its sudden impact brings—the abrupt disclosure of the mountain summit, the wild cherry-tree in blossom, the crowning moment of a great concerto, witnessing to another beauty beyond sense. And again, any mature person looking back on their own past life, will be forced to recognise factors in that life, which cannot be attributed to heredity, environment, opportunity, personal initiative or mere chance. The contact which proved decisive, the path unexpectedly opened, the other path closed, the thing we felt compelled to say, the letter we felt compelled to write. It is as if a hidden directive power, personal, living, free, were working through circumstances and often against our intention or desire; pressing us in a certain direction, and moulding us to a certain design.

For meditation: Here is a force from beyond the world with disconcerting power.

For prayer: Again and again, Holy God, I seek to live my life on my own terms but again and again you break in to make me aware of your presence.

DECEMBER 6

A Plan of Life

It is this constant correlation between inward and outward that really matters; and this has always been the difficulty for human beings, because there are two natures in us, pulling different ways, and their reconciliation is a long and arduous task. Many people seem to think that the spiritual life necessarily requires a definite and exacting plan of study. It does not. But it does require a definite plan of life; and courage in sticking to the plan, not merely for days or weeks, but for years. New mental and emotional habits must be formed, all our interests re-arranged in new proportion round a new centre. This is something which cannot be hurried; but, unless we take it seriously, can be infinitely delayed. Many people suggest by their behaviour that God is of far less importance than their bath, morning paper, or early cup of tea. The life of co-operation with Him must begin with a full and practical acceptance of the truth that God alone matters; and that He, the Perfect, always desires perfection. Then it will inevitably press us to begin working for perfection; first in our own characters and actions, next in our homes, surroundings, profession and country. We must be prepared for the fact that even on small and personal levels this will cost a good deal; frequently thwarting our own inclinations and demanding real sacrifice.

Here the further question of the relation of spiritual life to public life and politics comes in. It must mean, for all who take it seriously, judging public issues from the angle of eternity, never from that of national self-interest or expediency; backing our conviction, as against party of prejudice, rejecting compromise, and voting only for those who adopt this disinterested point of view. Did we act thus, slowly but surely a body of opinion—a spiritual party, if you like—might be formed; and in the long run make its influence felt in the State. But such a programme demands much faith, hope, and charity; and courage too.

For meditation: God . . . always desires perfection.

For prayer: In the midst of angry voices and divisions, help me, Sovereign God, to seek only your will and to persevere in working for your justice and peace in my own life and in all life.

DECEMBER 7

God's Agents in the Real World

We are the agents of the Creative Spirit in this world. Real advance in the spiritual life, then, means accepting this vocation with all it involves. Not merely turning over the pages of an engineering magazine and enjoying the pictures, but putting on overalls and getting on with the job. The real spiritual life must be horizontal as well as vertical; spread more and more. It must be larger, richer, fuller, more generous in its interests than the interests of the natural life alone can ever be; must invade and transform all homely activities and practical things. For it means an offering of life to the Father of life, to Whom it belongs; a willingness—an eager willingness—to take our small place in the vast operations of His Spirit instead of trying to run a poky little business on our own.

So now we come back to this ordinary mixed life of every day, in which we find ourselves—the life of house and work, tube and aeroplane, newspaper and cinema, wireless and television, with its tangle of problems and suggestions and demands—and consider what we are to do about that; how, within its homely limitations, we can co-operate with the Will. It is far easier, though not very easy, to develop and preserve a spiritual outlook on life, than it is to make our everyday actions harmonise with that spiritual outlook. That means trying to see things, persons and choices from the angle of eternity; and dealing with them as part of the material in which the Spirit works. This will be decisive for the way we behave as to our personal, social, and national obligations. It will decide the papers we read, the movements we support, the kind of administrators we vote for, our attitude to social and international justice. For though we may renounce the world for ourselves, refuse the attempt to get anything out of it, we have to accept it as the sphere in which we are to co-operate with the Spirit, and try to do the Will. Therefore the prevalent notion that spirituality and politics have nothing to do with one another is the exact opposite of the truth. Once it is accepted in a realistic sense, the Spiritual Life has everything to do with politics. It means that certain convictions about God and the world become the moral and spiritual imperatives of our life; and this must be decisive for the way we choose to behave about that bit of the world over which we have been given a limited control.

For meditation: [We need] to see . . . persons and choices from the angle of eternity.

For prayer: Knowing that you are at work in human history to accomplish your purpose and to establish your reign, let my life become an instrument of your purpose and enable me to seek and serve that purpose in all that I do.

December 8

Spiritual Life

A genuine inner life must make us more and more sensitive to that moulding power, working upon His creation at every level, not at one alone: and especially to the constant small but expert touches, felt in and through very homely events, upon those half-made, unsteady souls which are each the subject of His detailed care. A real artist will give as much time and trouble to a miniature two inches square, as to the fresco on the Cathedral wall. The true splendour and heart-searching beauty of the Divine Charity is not seen in those cosmic energies which dazzle and confound us; but in the transcendent power which stoops to an intimate and cherishing love, the grave and steadfast Divine action, sometimes painful and sometimes gentle, on the small unfinished soul. . . .

We are so busy rushing about, so immersed in what we call practical things, that we seldom pause to realize the mysterious truth of our situation: how little we know that really matters, how completely our modern knowledge leaves the deeps of our existence unexplored. We are inclined to leave all that out. . . . Christ never left it out. His teaching has a deep recurrent note of awe, a solemn sense of God and the profound mysteries of God: His abrupt creative entrance into every human life, coming to us, touching us, changing us in every crisis, grief, shock, sacrifice, flashing up on life's horizon like lightning just when we had settled down on the natural level, and casting over the landscape a light we had never dreamed of before. The whole teaching of Christ hinges on the deep mystery and awful significance of our existence; and God, as the supreme and ever-present factor in every situation, from the tiniest to the most universal. The span of His understanding goes from the lilies of the field to the most terrible movements of history. He takes in all the darkness and anxiety of our situation, whether social or personal; and within and beyond all, He finds the creative action of God, the one Reality, the one Life, working with a steadfast and unalterable love, sometimes by the direct action of circumstance and sometimes secretly within each soul in prayer. And this creative action, so hidden and so penetrating, is the one thing that matters in human life.

For meditation: God is . . . the supreme and ever-present factor in every situation.

For prayer: You are present, Eternal God, in every moment of my life, in the daily tasks and in the swirl and seeming chaos of world events; help me then to be aware of your presence and responsive to your purpose.

December 9

A Job to Be Done

More is required of those who wake up to reality, than the passive adoration of God or intimate communion with God. Those responses, great as they are, do not cover the purpose of our creation. The riches and beauty of the spiritual landscape are not disclosed to us in order that we may sit in the sun parlour, be grateful for the excellent hospitality, and contemplate the glorious view. Some people suppose that the spiritual life mainly consists in doing that. God provides the spectacle. We gaze with reverent appreciation from our comfortable seats, and call this proceeding Worship.

No idea of our situation could be more mistaken than this. Our place is not the auditorium but the stage—or, as the case may be, the field, workshop, study, laboratory—because we ourselves form part of the creative apparatus of God, or at least are meant to form part of the creative apparatus of God. He made us in order to use us, and use us in the most profitable way; for His purpose, not ours. To live a spiritual life means subordinating all other interests to that single fact. Sometimes our positions seem to be that of tools; taken up when wanted, used in ways which we had not expected for an object on which our opinion is not asked, and then laid down. Sometimes we are the currency used in some great operation, of which the purpose is not revealed to us. Sometimes we are servants, left year in, year out to the same monotonous job. Sometimes we are conscious fellow-workers with the Perfect, striving to bring the Kingdom in. But whatever our particular place or job may be, it means the austere conditions of the workshop, not the free-lance activities of the messy but well-meaning amateur; clocking in at the right time and tending the machine in the right way. Sometimes, perhaps, carrying on for years with a machine we do not very well understand and do not enjoy; because it needs doing, and no one else is available. Or accepting the situation quite quietly, when a job we felt that we were managing excellently is taken away. Taking responsibility if we are called to it, or just bringing the workers their dinner, cleaning and sharpening the tools. All self-willed choices and obstinacy drained out of what we thought to be our work; so that it becomes more and more God's work in us.

For meditation: God made us in order to use us . . . for God's purpose, not ours.

For prayer: I cannot always see or know your purpose, Gracious Creator, so help me to grow more trusting and to let you shape my life toward your purpose.

DECEMBER 10

Centering

Most of our conflicts and difficulties come from trying to deal with the spiritual and practical aspects of our life separately instead of realising them as parts of one whole. If our practical life is centred on our own interests, cluttered up by possessions, distracted by ambitions, passions, wants and worries, beset by a sense of our own rights and importance, or anxieties for our own future, or longings for our own success, we need not expect that our spiritual life will be a contrast to all this. The soul's house is not built on such a convenient plan: there are few sound-proof partitions in it. Only when the conviction—not merely the idea—that the demand of the Spirit, however inconvenient, comes first and IS first, rules the whole of it, will those objectionable noises die down which have a way of penetrating into the nicely furnished little oratory, and drowning all the quieter voices by their din.

St. John of the Cross, in a famous and beautiful poem, described the beginning of the journey of his soul to God:

> "In an obscure night
> Fevered by Love's anxiety
>   O hapless, happy plight
> I went, none seeing me,
> Forth from my house, where all things quiet be."

Not many of us could say that. Yet there is no real occasion for tumult, strain, conflict, anxiety, once we have reached the living conviction that God is All. All takes place within Him. He alone matters, He alone is. Our spiritual life is His affair; because, whatever we may think to the contrary, it is really produced by His steady attraction, and our humble and self-forgetful response to it. It consists in being drawn, at His pace and in His way, to the place where He wants us to be; not the place we fancied for ourselves.

For meditation: All takes place within [God].

For prayer: In the dailiness of life, my Guide and my Goal, teach me that this also is to be offered, teach me to place all things in your hands in confidence and peaceful trust.

DECEMBER 11

Evil and Reality

When we consider the evil, injustice, and misery existing in the world, how can we claim that the ultimate Reality at the heart of the universe is a Spirit of peace, harmony, and infinite love? What evidence can we bring to support such a belief? And how can we adore a God whose creation is marred by cruelty, suffering and sin?

This is, of course, the problem of evil; the crucial problem for all realistic religion. It is no use to dodge this issue, and still less use to pretend that the Church has a solution of the problem up her sleeve. I would rather say with Baron von Hügel that Christian spirituality does not explain evil and suffering, which remain a mystery beyond the reach of the human mind, but does show us how to deal with them. It insists that something has gone wrong, and badly wrong, with the world. That world as we know it does not look like the work of the loving Father whom the Gospels call us to worship; but rather, like the work of selfish and undisciplined children who have been given wonderful material and a measure of freedom, and not used that freedom well. Yet we see in this muddled world a constant struggle for Truth, Goodness, Perfection; and all those who give themselves to that struggle—the struggle for the redemption of the world from greed, cruelty, injustice, selfish desire and their results—find themselves supported and reinforced by a spiritual power which enhances life, strengthens will, and purifies character. And they come to recognise more and more in that power the action of God. These facts are as real as the other facts, which distress and puzzle us; the apparent cruelty, injustice and futility of life. We have to account somehow for the existence of gentleness, purity, self-sacrifice, holiness, love; and how can we account for them, unless they are attributes of Reality?

For meditation: There is a spiritual power which enhances life.

For prayer: Help me, Good and gracious God, in the midst of this muddled world to take my part in the struggle against greed and injustice and selfishness and rely on your strength in the struggle for purity, holiness, and love.

DECEMBER 12

Facing Reality as Baptized Christians

You and I are committed, as baptized Christians, to what has been given His deep and touching earthly revelation, to the steady loyal effort, in our own small place and way, towards bringing that mounting vision a little nearer completeness, bringing a little more of that Kingdom in. Each faithful upward glance, each movement of trust, each act of selfless love, helps it on. . . . The Hallowing of the whole Universe, physical, mental and spiritual in all its grades, the infinitely great and the infinitely small, giving our lives at whatever cost to the helping of the fulfilment of their sacramental promise—we must take sides in some way for that, because we are the Children of God.

Those thoughts kill all self-occupied fuss. They brace and delight us, remind us that our religion is not a refuge from Reality, it is a demand that we face Reality with all its difficulties, opportunities, implications; that we face God and His whole mysterious purpose and our own solemn responsibility to Him.

When Christ said, "My Father and your Father, My God and your God," He said it not in the easy way we repeat what we think a consoling text. *Is* it consoling? Is it not tremendous, searching? Does it not ask for a tremendous response? We know what His own response was like and what it entailed. Was He not making a declaration which must transfigure the whole lives of those who realize all that is implied in it? Sweeping them into a closer union with His vision and joy and sufferings? Conferring on them the tremendous privilege of partnership?

Fellow-workers with God because co-heirs with Christ. Do let us take that literally! "Christ," says de Caussade, "calls us all to perfection because He calls us all to submit to the Will of the Father and this is the same thing as Perfection." It is the complete acceptance of our life as Children of God, part of His creative purpose; it is "being made the Children of God and of the Light" as the baptismal service has it.

For meditation: God confers on us the tremendous privilege of partnership.

For prayer: If you call on me Lord God, to work in partnership with you, grant me also the wisdom to know your will and the strength to serve you.

DECEMBER 13

Christ Changes Circumstances

More and more as we go on with the Christian life we learn the strange power of the Spirit over circumstance; seldom sensationally declared but always present and active—God in His richness and freedom coming as a factor into every situation, overruling the ceaseless stream of events which make up our earthly existence and, through those events, moulding our souls. The radiation of His love penetrates, modifies, quickens our lives.

This general action of the Power of God in life is what we rather vaguely call Providence. Its pressure and action is continuous in and through the texture of that life but usually it is unseen. It conditions our whole career from birth to death just as the invisible lines of force within a magnetic field condition all the tiny iron filings scattered on it. But now and then it does emerge on the surface and startles us by its witness to a subtle and ceaseless power and love working within the web of events. I am sure we ought to think of this far more than we do. When instances of its action are collected as in *The Holy and the Living God* (by M. D. R.Willink) we are astonished at their impressiveness. This sort of evidence of the direct action of God lies very thick on the pages of the New Testament, sometimes intervening in great and crucial events, sometimes in very homely things like the shortage of wine at the wedding made good and the situation saved, sometimes in desperate crises like the storm quelled just in time, the chosen servants of God brought safely through danger, the prison doors opened.

"The power of God unto salvation," says St. Paul (not the power of God unto comfort) is the essence of the Gospel, a personal energy, a never-ceasing Presence that intervenes and overrules events.

I don't know why we think this strange. It is just our dull unimaginative stuffiness. Even on our tiny human scale, we feel that the perfect master of a great industry is one who organizes the whole in the interest of good and profitable work and of the well-being of the workers, who gives his subordinates a relative freedom and lets the factory run on ordained lines without too much interference in details. Yet he is always accessible to the personal troubles and desires of his workers, overrides roles where necessary and is interested in every detail down to the factory cat. Even one human creature can do that without surprising us. But when Christ says the Absolute Majesty and Holiness of God can both rule heaven and care for the sparrow and will intervene to help and save, we think that is poetry and paradox, and stories about it are superstitions. We are too stupid and too narrow in our notions to conceive the energy of the Unmeasurable Holy, entering our world, changing and modifying circumstance.

For meditation: The essence of the Gospel . . . [is] a never-ceasing Presence that intervenes and overrules events.

For prayer: Beyond my ability to see or understand, Eternal God, is your never-ceasing Presence transforming daily events; help me to open myself more fully to your transforming grace and to become more often an instrument of your purpose.

DECEMBER 14

Corporate Life and Mysticism

As the life and growth of the Church proceed, her corporate consciousness, enriched by all the discoveries of the saints, grows richer: so that she has more and more to give to each of her sons. The beautiful interdependence of all Christian souls, living and dead, everything that is meant by the doctrine of the "Communion of Saints," is here strongly illustrated, and refutes the common idea that mysticism is individualistic, and can nourish independently of history or tradition. Thus all Christian mysticism is soaked in the language and ideas of the Bible; is perpetually taught and re-taught by St. Paul and St. John. In addition to this, it reflects the special religious colour of the period to which it belongs, and hands on to a later time the spiritual treasures extracted from it. The Catholic mystics of the Middle Ages have the peculiar beauties of their epoch, and frequently in their sayings remind us of the very spirit of Gothic art. After the Reformation, another mood and attitude predominate, yet the link with the past is not really broken. Even such one-sided mystics as the Quakers, who hold that all truth is revealed directly by the Inner Light of God in the soul, or the Quietists, who try to wait in a blank state of passivity for His message, still depend for their most characteristic notions on the deep common beliefs of Christendom concerning God and His communion with the spirit of man.

The corporate side of Christian mysticism has therefore great importance. If we want really to understand its literature, its history, and especially its psychology, we cannot afford to neglect the influence of that great and growing body of spiritual truth on which, knowingly or not, each successive mystic feeds his soul. In all religious experience, a large part is and must be played by that which psychologists call "apperception." By apperception is meant the fact that there are in all our experiences two distinct factors. There is first the apprehension, the message, which comes to us from the outside world; secondly there are the ideas, images and memories already present in our minds, which we involuntarily combine with the message, and by which we develop, modify or explain it. Now this mixture of perceptions and memories obviously takes place in all mystical experience. The mind which the mystic brings to his encounter with God is not a blank sheet. On the contrary, it is generally richly furnished with religious ideas and metaphors, and trained to special kinds of religious practices, all of which help him to actualize the more or less obscure apprehensions of Eternal Truth that come to him in his contemplations. Were it not so, he could hardly tell us anything of that which he has felt and known. Thus it is that certain symbols and phrases—for instance, the Fire of Love, the Spiritual Marriage, the Inward Light, the classic stages of the soul's ascent—occur again and again in the writings of the mystics, and suggest to us the substantial unity of their experiences. These phrases lead us back to the historical background within which these mystics emerge; and remind us that they are, like other Christians, members of one another, and living (though with a peculiar intensity) the life to which all Christians are called.

For meditation: We are members of one another.

For prayer: Holy and gracious God, you have enriched your church with special gifts of mystical insight; help us to make full use of those gifts to deepen our own lives and so to draw others also to a growing knowledge of your unsearchable love.

December 15

Centrality of Prayer

If the seeking of the Eternal is actuated by love, the finding of it is
achieved through prayer. Prayer, in fact—understood as a life or state,
not an act or an asking—is the beginning, middle and end of all that
we are now considering. As the social self can only be developed by
contact with society, so the spiritual self can only be developed by
contact with the spiritual world. And such humble yet ardent contact
with the spiritual world—opening up to its suggestions our impulses,
our reveries, our feelings, our most secret dispositions as well as our
mere thoughts—is the essence of prayer, understood in its widest
sense. No more than surrender or love can such prayer be reduced to
"one act." Those who seek to sublimate it into "pure" contemplation
are as limited at one end of the scale, as those who reduce it to articu-
late petition are at the other. It contains in itself a rich variety of
human reactions and experiences. It opens the door upon an
unwalled world, in which the self truly lives and therefore makes
widely various responses to its infinitely varying stimuli. Into that
world the self takes, or should take, its special needs, aptitudes and
longings, and matches them against its apprehension of Eternal Truth.
In this meeting of the human heart with all that it can apprehend of
Reality, not adoration alone but unbounded contrition, not humble
dependence alone but joy, peace and power, not rapture alone but
mysterious darkness, must be woven into the fabric of love. In this
world the soul may sometimes wander as if in pastures, sometimes is

poised breathless and intent. Sometimes it is fed by beauty, sometimes by most difficult truth, and experiences the extremes of riches and destitution, darkness and light. "It is not," says Plotinus, "by crushing the Divine into a unity but by displaying its exuberance, as the Supreme Himself has displayed it, that we show knowledge of the might of God."

Thus, by that instinctive and warmly devoted direction of its behaviour which is love, and that willed attention to and communion with the spiritual world which is prayer, all the powers of the self are united and turned towards the seeking and finding of the Eternal. It is by complete obedience to this exacting love, doing difficult and unselfish things, giving up easy and comfortable things—in fact by living, living hard on the highest levels—that men more and more deeply feel experience, and enter into their spiritual life.

For meditation: It is by complete obedience [that we enter] spiritual life.

For prayer: Let your love for me, Loving and gracious God, awaken such love for you that I may turn toward you more fully and live the life to which you call me.

DECEMBER 16

Spiritual Life Begins with Prayer

God, not man, is the first term of religion: and our first step in religion is the acknowledgment that He Is. All else is the unfolding of those truths about His life and our life, which this fact of facts involves. I believe in One God. We begin there; not with our own needs, desires, feelings, or obligations. Were all these abolished, His independent splendour would remain, as the Truth which gives its meaning to the world. So we begin by stating with humble delight our belief and trust in the most concrete, most rich of all realities—God. Yet even the power to do this reflects back again to Him, and witnesses to His self-giving to the soul. For Christianity is not a pious reverie, a moral system or a fantasy life; it is a revelation, adapted to our capacity, of the Realities which control life. Those Realities must largely remain unknown to us; limited little creatures that we are. God, as Brother Giles said, is a great mountain of corn from which man, like a sparrow, takes a grain of wheat: yet even that grain of wheat, which is as much as we can carry away, contains all the essentials of our life. We are to carry it carefully and eat it gratefully: remembering with awe the majesty of the mountain from which it comes. The first thing this vast sense of God does for us, is to deliver us from the imbecilities of religious self-love and self-assurance; and sink our little souls in the great life of the race, in and upon which this One God in His mysterious independence is always working, whether we notice it or not. When that sense of His unique reality gets dim and stodgy, we must go back and begin there once more; saying with the Psalmist, "All my fresh springs are in thee." Man, said Christ, is nourished by every word that proceeds out of the mouth of God. Not the words we expect, or persuade ourselves that we have heard; but those unexpected words He really utters, sometimes by the mouths of the most unsuitable people, sometimes through apparently unspiritual events, sometimes secretly within the soul. Therefore seeking God, and listening to God, is an important part of the business of human life: and this is the essence of prayer. We do something immense, almost unbelievable, when we enter that world of prayer, for then we deliberately move out towards that transcendent Being whom Christianity declares to be the one Reality: a Reality revealed to us in three ways as a Creative Love, a Rescuing Love, and an Indwelling, all-pervading Love, and in each of those three ways claiming and responding to our absolute trust. Prayer is the give-and-take between the little souls of men and that three-fold Reality.

For meditation: Our first step in religion is the acknowledgment that God Is.

For prayer: Grant me, Almighty God of Love, the humility to remember always the mystery beyond my understanding and to seek, not so much to understand, as to worship.

December 17

Prayer Is Central

Prayer means turning to Reality, taking our part, however humble, tentative and half-understood, in the continual conversation, the communion, of our spirits with the Eternal Spirit; the acknowledgment of our entire dependence, which is yet the partly free dependence of the child. For Prayer is really our whole life toward God: our longing for Him, our "incurable God-sickness," as Barth calls it, our whole drive towards Him. It is the humble correspondence of the human spirit with the Sum of all Perfection, the Fountain of Life. No narrower definition than this is truly satisfactory, or covers all the ground. Here we are, small half-real creatures of sense and spirit, haunted by the sense of a Perfection ever calling to us, and yet ourselves so fundamentally imperfect, so hopelessly involved in an imperfect world; with a passionate desire for beauty, and more mysteriously still, a knowledge of beauty, and yet unable here to realise perfect beauty; with a craving for truth and a deep reverence for truth, but only able to receive flashes of truth. Yet we know that perfect goodness, perfect beauty, and perfect truth exist within the Life of God; and that our hearts will never rest in less than these. This longing, this need of God, however dimly and vaguely we feel it, is the seed from which grows the strong, beautiful and fruitful plant of prayer. It is the first response of our deepest selves to the attraction of the Perfect; the recognition that He has made us for Himself, that we depend on Him and are meant to depend on Him, and that we shall not know the meaning of peace until our communion with Him is at the centre of our lives.

"Without Thee, I cannot live." Whatever our small practice, belief, or experience may be, nothing can alter the plain fact that God, the Spirit of spirits, the Life-giving Life, has made or rather is making each person reading these words for Himself; and that our lives will not achieve stability until they are ruled by that truth. All creation has purpose. It looks towards perfection. "In the volume of the book it is written of me, that I should fulfil thy will, O God." Not in some mysterious spiritual world that I know nothing about; but here and now, where I find myself, as a human creature of spirit and of sense, immersed in the modern world—subject to time with all its vicissitudes, and yet penetrated by the Eternal, and finding reality not in one but in both. To acknowledge and take up that double obligation to the seen and the unseen, in however homely and practical a way, is to enter consciously upon the spiritual life. That will mean time and attention given to it; a deliberate drawing-in from the circumference to the centre, that "setting of life in order" for which St. Thomas Aquinas prayed.

For meditation: All creation has purpose.

For prayer: Increase my restless longing for your presence in my life, my Creator and Redeemer; set my life in order and direct me toward your perfect truth.

DECEMBER 18

Prayer Gives Our Lives Focus

When we lift our eyes from the crowded by-pass to the eternal hills; then, how much the personal and practical things we have to deal with are enriched. What meaning and coherence come into our scattered lives. We mostly spend those lives conjugating three verbs: to Want, to Have, and to Do. Craving, clutching, and fussing, on the material, political, social, emotional, intellectual—even on the religious— plane, we are kept in perpetual unrest: forgetting that none of these verbs have any ultimate significance, except so far as they are tran- scended by and included in, the fundamental verb, to Be: and that Being, not wanting, having and doing, is the essence of a spiritual life. But now, with this widening of the horizon, our personal ups and downs, desires, cravings, efforts, are seen in scale; as small and transitory spiritual facts, within a vast, abiding spiritual world, and lit by a steady spiritual light. And at once a new coherence comes into our existence, a new tranquility and release. Like a chalet in the Alps, that homely existence gains atmosphere, dignity, significance from the greatness of the sky above it, and the background of the everlasting hills.

The people of our time are helpless, distracted and rebellious, unable to interpret that which is happening, and full of apprehension about that which is to come, largely because they have lost this sure hold on the eternal; which gives to each life meaning and direction, and with meaning and direction gives steadiness. I do not mean by this a mere escape from our problems and dangers, a slinking away from the actual to enjoy the eternal. I mean an acceptance and living out of the actual, in its homeliest details and its utmost demands, in the light of the eternal; and with that peculiar sense of ultimate security which only a hold on the eternal brings. When the vivid reality which is meant by these rather abstract words is truly possessed by us, when that which is unchanging in ourselves is given its chance, and emerges from the stream of succession to recognise its true home and goal, which is God—then, though much suffering may, indeed will remain, apprehension, confusion, instability, despair, will cease.

For meditation: Being, not wanting, having and doing, is the essence of a spiritual life.

For prayer: Let your eternal light, Lord God, show me the world as it really is so that I may live each day in confidence, sure that each moment has eternal meaning and that your love pervades all things.

DECEMBER 19

Life of Prayer

[Think of] the span and the depth which is required of a full Christian life of prayer. For one part of prayer associates us with that creative and supporting Love, and requires us to give ourselves as open channels through which it can be poured out on all life; and the other part of prayer keeps us in humble awareness of our own complete dependence, plastic to the pressure of the moulding Charity. When we consider our situation like this, we realize that the very best we are likely to achieve in the world of prayer will be a small part in a mighty symphony; not a peculiarly interesting duet. When our devotional life seems to us to have become a duet, we should listen more carefully. Then we shall hear a greater music, within which that little melody of ours can find its place.

This truth of the deep unity of creation links us with our lesser relations, and with our greater relations too. It makes us the members of a family, a social order, so rich and various that we can never exhaust its possibilities. . . . We are all serving on one Staff. Our careful pickings and choosings, acceptances and exclusions, likes and dislikes, race prejudice, class prejudice, and all the rest, look rather silly within the glow of that One God, in Whom all live and move and have their being; and the graduated splendour of that creation which is the work of His paternal Love. . . . It insists upon our own utter dependence on the constant, varied, unseen Creative Love; and the narrow span of our understanding of our fellow creatures—how slight is the material we have for passing judgment on them—because our understanding is no wider than our charity.

And now we come down to the more painful consideration of all that this demands from us, if our inner and outer life are to match our belief about Reality; and only when this has happened will Christianity conquer the world, harmonizing all things visible and invisible because both are received and loved as the works of One God. There are still far too many Christians in whose souls a sound-proof partition has been erected between the oratory and the kitchen: sometimes between the oratory and the Study too. But the creative action of the Spirit penetrates the whole of life, and is felt by us in all sorts of ways. If our idea of that creative action is so restricted that we fail to recognize it working within the homely necessities and opportunities of our visible life, we may well suspect the quality of those invisible experiences to which we like to give spiritual status. "I found Him very easily among the pots and pans," said St. Teresa. "The duties of my position take precedence of everything else," said Elizabeth Leseur, pinned down by those duties to a life which was a constant check on the devotional practices she loved. She recognized the totality of God's creative action, penetrating and controlling the whole web of life.

For meditation: The Spirit penetrates the whole of life.

For prayer: Do not let the limits of my understanding, Almighty God, limit your work within me nor my response to your presence in every moment of my life and every person around me.

DECEMBER 20

The Focus of Prayer

These great objective truths are not very fashionable among modern Christians; yet how greatly we need them, if we are to escape pettiness, individualism and emotional bias. For that mysterious inner life which glows at the heart of Christianity, which we recognize with delight whenever we meet it, and which is the source of Christian power in the world, is fed through two channels. Along one channel a certain limited knowledge of God and the things of God enters the mind; and asks of us that honest and humble thought about the mysteries of faith which is the raw material of meditation. Along the other channel God Himself comes secretly to the heart, and wakes up that desire and that sense of need which are the cause of prayer. The awestruck vision of faith and the confident movement of love are both needed, if the life of devotion is to be rich, brave and humble; equally removed from mere feeling and mere thought. Christian prayer to God must harmonize with Christian belief about God: and quickly loses humility and sanity if it gets away from that great law. We pray first because we believe something; perhaps at that stage a very crude or vague something. And with the deepening of prayer, its patient cultivation, there comes—perhaps slowly, perhaps suddenly—the enrichment and enlargement of belief, as we enter into a first-hand communion with the Reality who is the object of our faith. . . .

So we begin the overhaul of our spiritual equipment not by thinking about our own needs and shortcomings, but by looking up and out at this One Reality, this Unchanging God, and so gaining a standard of comparison, a "control." That remarkable naturalist and philosopher, Dr. Beebe, whose patient study of living things seems to have brought him so near to the sources of life, says in his latest book *Nonsuch*, "As a panacea for a host of human ills, worries and fears, I should like to advocate a law that every toothbrush should have a small telescope in its handle, and the two used equally." As far as the life of religion is concerned, if we always used the telescope before we used the toothbrush—looked first at the sky of stars, the great ranges of the beauty and majesty of God, and only then at our own small souls and their condition, needs, and sins—the essential work of the toothbrush would be much better done; and without that self-conscious conviction of its overwhelming importance, and the special peculiarities and requirements of our own set of teeth, which the angels must surely find amusing. "Where I left myself I found God; where I found myself, I lost God," says Meister Eckhart. Our eyes are not in focus for His Reality, until they are out of focus for our own petty concerns.

For meditation: We begin by looking up and out.

For prayer: Help me, Creator of the universe, always to remember the reality and infinite majesty of your Being and to live in humble gratitude for the equal reality of your love.

DECEMBER 21

Contemplation

Contemplation of Christ does not mean an emotional sort of pious daydream; it means entering by a deliberate, self-oblivious and humble attention into the tremendous mysteries of His Life—mysteries which each give us some deep truth about the life and Will of God and the power and vocation of a soul that is given to God—mysteries which each one of us in particular is called to make part of our very lives. They will break up, into colours we can deal with, that white light of God's Holiness at which we cannot look.

You know sometimes how one goes to see a church which one is told has magnificent windows—and seen from outside they all look alike—dull, thick, grubby. We probably say, "Well! it is obvious there is good glass here but we cannot realize it." Then we open the door and go inside—leave the outer world, enter the inner world—and the universal light floods through the windows and bathes us in their colour and beauty and significance, shows us things of which *we* had never dreamed, a loveliness that lies beyond the fringe of speech. And so in the same way we cannot realize God and all our Lord's lovely meaning as a revelation of God and His eternal Truth and Beauty, from outside. One constantly hears people commenting on Christianity from outside and missing the point every time. They are on the wrong side of the wall. How important then it is for us to be familiar with the inner vision. It is from within the place of prayer, recollection, worship and love, where the altar is, where the sacrifice is made, where we are all bound together in a life of communion and self-giving to God, that we fully and truly receive the revelation which is made through Christ. Then we see the different acts and stages of His life like a series of windows through which streams into our souls the pure light of God, mediated to us in a way we can bear: Eternity and Reality given to us in human terms. To re-enter that Cathedral, receive a fresh gift from its inexhaustible beauty, see through those windows more and more of the light of God, that is the secret of meditation. Julian says at the end of her *Revelations* that what she had received from her vision of Christ was "Light, Life and Love"; everything was gathered in that; an energy to show us the Truth, quicken us to fresh vitality and fill us with adoring devotion. What a contrast to our stodgy, vague, twilight inner life! We come into the silence to get more Light, Life and Love. We come to contemplate our Christian treasure from inside.

For meditation: We come into the silence to get more Light, Life and Love.

For prayer: Holy God, Infinite Mystery, source of all life and light and love, let me walk with you in my daily life, let me come toward you in my prayer, let me know you in your holy word, let me receive you at your altar, and let me live only in you both now and always.

DECEMBER 22

Love in Creation

"He shewed me a little thing," says Julian of Norwich, "the quantity of a hazel nut in the palm of my hand; and it was as round as a ball. I looked thereupon with the eye of my understanding and thought: *What may this be*? And it was answered generally thus: *It is all that is made*. . . . In this Little Thing I saw three properties. The first is that God made it, the second is that God loveth it, the third, that God keepeth it."

That is a saint's comment on the first article of her Creed. It is a vision that takes much living-out in a world in which injustice and greed are everywhere manifest; full too of tendencies which we are able to recognize as evil, and of misery and failure which seem the direct result of corporate stupidity and self-love, offering us ceaseless opportunities for the expression of disapproval and disgust, and often tempting to despair. "All-thing hath the Being by the Love of God," says Julian again. And then we think of a natural order shot through with suffering, marred at every point by imperfection, maintained by mutual destruction; a natural order which includes large populations of vermin, and the flora and fauna of infectious disease. It is easy to be both sentimental and theological over the more charming and agreeable aspects of Nature. It is very difficult to see its essential holiness beneath disconcerting and hostile appearances with an equable and purified sight; with something of the large, disinterested Charity of God.

To stand alongside the generous Creative Love, maker of all things visible and invisible (including those we do not like) and see them with the eyes of the Artist-Lover is the secret of sanctity. St. Francis did this with a singular perfection; but we know the price that he paid. So too that rapt and patient lover of all life, Charles Darwin, with his great, self-forgetful interest in the humblest and tiniest forms of life—not because they were useful to him, but for their own sakes—fulfilled one part of our Christian duty far better than many Christians do. It is a part of the life of prayer, which is our small attempt to live the life of Charity, to consider the whole creation with a deep and selfless reverence; enter into its wonder, and find in it the mysterious intimations of the Father of Life, maker of all things, Creative Love.

For meditation: [To] see [all things] with the eyes of the Artist-Lover is the secret of sanctity.

For prayer: Let all creation, Creator of all things, speak to me of your presence and deepen my prayer for all things and draw my prayer through all things to you the source and creator of all life and my life.

DECEMBER 23

Love Is an Orientation toward God

Christians, on the authority of their Master, declare that such love of God requires all that they have, not only of feeling, but also of intellect and of power; since He is to be loved with heart and mind and strength. Thought and action on highest levels are involved in it, for it means, not religious emotionalism, but the unflickering orientation of the whole self towards Him, ever seeking and finding the Eternal; the linking up of all behaviour on that string, so that the apparently hard and always heroic choices which are demanded, are made at last because they are inevitable. It is true that this dominant interest will give to our lives a special emotional colour and a special kind of happiness; but in this, as in the best, deepest, richest human love, such feeling-tone and such happiness—though in some natures of great beauty and intensity—are only to be looked upon as secondary characters, and never to be aimed at.

When St. Teresa said that the real object of the spiritual marriage was "the incessant production of work, work," I have no doubt that many of her nuns were disconcerted; especially the type of ease-loving conservatives whom she and her intimates were accustomed to refer to as the pussy-cats. But in this direct application to religious experience of St. Thomas' doctrine of love, she set up an ideal of the spiritual life which is as valid at the present day in the entanglements of our social order, as it was in the enclosed convents of sixteenth-century Spain. Love, we said, is the cause of action. It urges and directs

53

our behaviour, conscious and involuntary, towards an end. The mother is irresistibly impelled to act towards her child's welfare, the ambitious man towards success, the artist towards expression of his vision. All these are examples of behaviour, love-driven towards ends. And religious experience discloses to us a greater, more inclusive end, and this vital power of love as capable of being used on the highest levels, regenerated, directed to eternal interests; subordinating behaviour, inspiring suffering, unifying the whole self and its activities, mobilizing them for this transcendental achievement. This generous love . . . will indeed cause the behaviour it controls to exhibit both rightful contact with and renunciation of the particular and fleeting; because in and through this series of linked deeds it is uniting with itself all human activities, and in and through them is seeking and finding its eternal end. So, in that rightful bringing-in of novelty which is the business of the fully living soul, the most powerful agent is love, understood as the controlling factor of behaviour, the sublimation and union of will and desire.

For meditation: Love of God requires all that [we] have.

For prayer: Eternal Love, present in all life and seeking my life, override my selfish fears and defenses and turn all my thoughts and actions toward your purpose for me and for all this world.

DECEMBER 24

The Vision of Love

When we look out towards this Love that moves the stars and stirs in the child's heart, and claims our total allegiance and remember that this alone is Reality and we are only real so far as we conform to its demands, we see our human situation from a fresh angle; and perceive that it is both more humble and dependent, and more splendid, than we had dreamed. We are surrounded and penetrated by great spiritual forces, of which we hardly know anything. Yet the outward events of our life cannot be understood, except in their relation to that unseen and intensely living world, the Infinite Charity which penetrates and supports us, the God whom we resist and yet for whom we thirst; who is ever at work, transforming the self-centred desire of the natural creature into the wide-spreading, outpouring love of the citizen of Heaven.

If the Reality of God were small enough to be grasped, it would not be great enough to be adored; and so our holiest privilege would go. "I count not myself to have grasped; but as one that has been grasped, I press on," says St. Paul. But if all real knowledge here is a humbly delighted knowledge of our own ignorance—if, as the dying artist said, "The word we shall use most when we get to heaven will be 'Oh!'"—still we can realize something of what it means, to consider our world from this point of view. It means that everything we are given to deal with—including ourselves and our psychological material, however intractable—is the result of the creative action of a personal Love, who despises nothing that He has made. We, then, cannot take the risk of despising anything; and any temptation to do so must be attributed to our ignorance, stupidity or self-love, and recognized as something which distorts our vision of Reality.

For meditation: Everything we are given to deal with . . . is the result of the creative action of a personal Love.

For prayer: Come to us, Holy and Infinite God; be for us a Reality "small enough to be grasped" and yet "great enough to be adored"; expand our small hearts to make room for your unlimited love and reign in all human hearts as the Prince of Peace.

DECEMBER 25—CHRISTMAS DAY

Incarnation and Childhood

We are being shown here something profoundly significant about human life—"God speaks in a Son," a Baby Son, and reverses all our pet values. He speaks in our language and shows us His secret beauty on our scale. We have got to begin not by an arrogant other-worldliness, but by a humble recognition that human things can be very holy, very full of God, and that high-minded speculations about His nature need not be holy at all; that all life is engulfed in Him and He can reach out to us anywhere at any level.

As the Christmas Day Gospel takes us back to the Mystery of the Divine Nature—*In the beginning was the Word* . . .—so let us begin by thinking of what St. Catharine called the "Ocean Pacific of the God-head" enveloping all life. The depth and richness of His being are entirely unknown to us, poor little scraps as we are! And yet the unlimited Life who is Love right through—who loves and is wholly present where He loves, on every plane and at every point—so loved the world as to desire to give His thought, the deepest secrets of His heart to this small, fugitive, imperfect creation—to *us*. That seems immense.

And then the heavens open and what is disclosed? A Baby, God manifest in the flesh. The stable, the manger, the straw; poverty, cold, darkness—these form the setting of the Divine Gift. In this Child God gives His supreme message to the soul—Spirit to spirit—but in a human way. Outside in the fields the heavens open and the shepherds look up astonished to find the music and radiance of Reality all

around them. But inside, our closest contact with that same Reality is
being offered to us in the very simplest, homeliest way—emerging
right into our ordinary life. A baby—just that. We are not told that the
Blessed Virgin Mary saw the Angels or heard the *Gloria* in the air. Her
initiation had been quite different, like a quiet voice speaking in our
deepest prayer—"The Lord is with thee!" "Behold the handmaid of
the Lord." Humble self-abandonment is quite enough to give us God.

For meditation: Human things can be very holy.

For prayer: Come, Holy One; come, my Redeemer; come, Lord Jesus,
and be born in me, live in me, grow in me, until my life is transformed by your life and I seek only to know your love and make your
love known.

December 26—St. Stephen

Incarnation

Not long ago, I was standing in an artist's studio before an altar-piece which she had just made. It represented the Nativity: or rather, the eternal incarnation of the Holy, self-given for the world. In the foreground one saw the Blessed Virgin, its ordained instrument, and St. Joseph, watching by her bed. There was a patient grave simplicity about them both; reflected in the serious young angels, whose majestic scale suggested the greatness of that world of spirit from which they had been drawn. Below, the sheep were feeding very quietly too: innocent nature entirely at home among the mysteries of the supernatural order, one lamb turning from its mother to press more closely to the Mother of the Lamb of God. And behind the Blessed Virgin, the focus of the mystery, the link as it were between two worlds, the Child lay peacefully and helplessly on a small stone altar, as on a bed. The stillness of an eternal event brooded over the whole. I spoke to the artist of the beauty of this ancient conception; and she answered, "Yes, laid on the altar straight away. I like that. There's something so sturdy about it."

Our modern religion hardly makes enough of this element in the mystery of the Divine revelation; in His pattern declared to humanity, or in the life of prayer. Yet sturdiness, shouldering the burden and accepting the tension inevitable to all great undertakings—getting to grips with the dread problems of life, and the cost of all redemptive action—comes nearer than any fervour to the Mind of Christ, and the demands of Charity. It is comparatively easy for devout minds to feel moved, contrite, exalted, adoring; much more difficult to discount all feeling, and be sturdy about it. Christ was trained in a carpenter's shop; and we persist in preferring a confectioner's shop. But the energy of rescue, the outpouring of sacrificial love, which the supernatural life demands, is not to be got from a diet of devotional meringues and eclairs. The whole life made an oblation from the first—placed on the altar, and lived right through as a reasonable sacrifice from beginning to end—this is the pattern put before us. Only thus can humanity use to the full its strange power of embodying eternal realities; and uniting the extremes of mystery and homeliness.

For meditation: The whole life—placed on the altar—this is the pattern.

For prayer: At Bethlehem as in St. Stephen, Holy Savior, you have shown us the offering of our human life; grant that my life also may be fully offered in your service.

DECEMBER 27

Maturing

All gardeners know the importance of good root development before we force the leaves and flowers. So our life in God should be deeply rooted and grounded before we presume to expect to produce flowers and fruits; otherwise we risk shooting up into one of those lanky plants which can never do without a stick. We are constantly beset by the notion that we ought to perceive ourselves springing up quickly, like the seed on stony ground; show striking signs of spiritual growth. But perhaps we are only required to go on quietly, making root, growing nice and bushy; docile to the great slow rhythm of life. When we see no startling marks of our own religious progress or our usefulness to God, it is well to remember the baby in the stable and the little boy in the streets of Nazareth. The very life was there present, which was to change the whole history of the human race; the rescuing action of God. At that stage there was not much to show for it; yet there is perfect continuity between the stable and the Easter garden, and the thread that unites them is the hidden Will of God. The childish prayer of Nazareth was the right preparation for the awful prayer of the Cross.

So it is that the life of the Spirit is to unfold gently and steadily within us; till at the last the full stature for which God designed us is attained. It is an organic process, a continuous Divine action; not a sudden miracle or a series of jerks. Therefore there should be no struggle, impatience, self-willed effort in our prayer and self-discipline; but rather a great flexibility, a homely ordered life, a gentle acceptance of what comes to us, and a still gentler acceptance of the fact that much we see in others is still out of our own reach. The prayer of the growing spirit should be free, humble, simple; full of confidence and full of initiative too. The mystics constantly tell us, that the goal of this prayer and of the hidden life which shall itself become more and more of a prayer, is union with God. We meet this phrase often: far too often, for we lose the wholesome sense of its awfulness. What does union with God mean? Not a nice feeling which we enjoy in devout moments. This may or may not be a by-product of union with God; probably not. It can never be its substance. Union with God means such an entire self-giving to the Divine Charity, such identification with its interests, that the whole of our human nature is transformed in God, irradiated by His absolute light, His sanctifying grace. Thus it is woven up into the organ of His creative activity, His redeeming purpose; conformed to the pattern of Christ, heart, soul, mind and strength. Each time this happens, it means that one more creature has achieved its destiny; and each soul in whom the life of the Spirit is born, sets out towards that goal.

For meditation: The goal . . . is union with God.

For prayer: So seldom, Omnipotent and In-dwelling Spirit, am I aware of your presence in my life, yet I have no life apart from you; give me the gift of confident trust in your presence, power, and purpose.

DECEMBER 28—HOLY INNOCENTS

The Example of the Christ Child

The mystics keep telling us that the goal of that prayer and the goal of that hidden life which should itself become more and more of a prayer, is "union with God." We use that phrase often, much too often to preserve the wholesome sense of its awe-fulness. For what does union with God mean? It is not a nice feeling we get in devout moments. That may or may not be a by-product of union—probably not. It can never be its substance. Union with God means every bit of our human nature transfigured in Christ, woven up into His creative life and activity, absorbed into His redeeming purpose, heart, soul, mind and strength. Each time it happens it means that one of God's creatures has achieved its destiny.

And if men and women want to know what that means in terms of human nature, what it costs and what it becomes, there is only one way—contemplation of the life of Christ. Then we see that we grow in wisdom and stature not just for our own sakes—just to become spiritual—but that His teaching, healing, life-giving power may possess us and work through us; that we may lose our own lives and find His life, be conformed to the Pattern shown in Him, conformed to the Cross. Those are the rich and costly demands and experiences that lie before us as we look at the Child setting up a standard for both simple and teamed, teaching the secrets of life; and what they ask from us on our side and from our prayer is a very great simplicity, self-oblivion, dependence and suppleness, a willingness and readiness to respond to life where it finds us and to wait, to grow and change, not according to our preconceived notions and ideas of pace, but according to the overruling Will and Pace of God.

For meditation: The goal is union with God.

For prayer: Why is it, Lord, that I try so hard to pull away from you? Why do I try so hard to avoid the destiny and purpose for which I was made? Help me, I pray, to remember why I am here and to open myself to your creative power.

DECEMBER 29

Incarnation

No amount of description really tells us anything about Holiness; but an encounter with it shames, amazes, convinces and delights us all at once. "Thou art the Christ!" says St. Peter. "My Lord and my God!" says St. Thomas. They recognize something from beyond the world: One who enters our mixed life in His perfect beauty; and accepts all the normal conditions of an existence which is so much at the mercy of seasons and weather, thirst and hunger, so afflicted by distresses we do not understand, so vexed by devils we cannot cast out and tainted by sins we cannot forget. Through all this that Figure is walking; radiating in and through every situation a selfless charity, an untiring interest and love. The Word has spoken; and spoken in the language of everyday life. And because of this, within that everyday life man always has access to God; and can never, at any point in his career claim ignorance of the drift of God's Will, even though his own duty and action may often be hard to decide. God is Charity; and the human race has one Lord, who is Incarnate Charity and carries through its utmost demands to the Altar and the Cross. Every decision, therefore, that the Christian takes in life will be controlled by the fact that it must be compatible with following Him. This means that no Christian life will avoid Calvary; though we may come to it by many different ways.

So, because Holiness has entered our world, and appeared in our nature, we know that men and women can become holy; and are bound, in spite of all discouragements, to take an optimistic view of human life. The Church is an undying family which has its face set towards Holiness, and is fed upon the food which can—if we let it—produce Holiness. As the queen bee is produced by being fed from childhood on "royal jelly," and thus becomes the parent of new life; so it is what the Christian is given, and what he assimilates of the supernatural food—not what he is by nature—which makes him grow up into the life-giving order of God. The final test of holiness is not seeming very different from other people, but being used to make other people very different; becoming the parent of new life.

For meditation: The final test of Holiness is being used to make others holy.

For prayer: Holy and life-giving Lord, you accept us as we are but call us to be what we could never have imagined; let us never forget the possibility you reveal or be content with less than what you have shown us.

DECEMBER 30

Nativity

Nothing in this story, perhaps, is more significant than the quietness and simplicity of its beginning. The birth of the Child, the Shepherds and the Magi, the little boy of Nazareth and his wonderful experience in the Temple, and the long quiet years in the carpenter's shop; there seems at first sight nothing very supernatural in these things. Indeed, one of the most convicting aspects of Christianity, if we try to see it in terms of our own day, is the contrast between its homely and inconspicuous beginnings and the holy powers it brought into the world. It keeps us in perpetual dread of despising small things, humble people, little groups. The Incarnation means that the Eternal God enters our common human life with all the energy of His creative love, to transform it, to exhibit to us its richness, its unguessed significance; speaking our language, and showing us His secret beauty on our own scale.

Thus the spiritual life does not begin in an arrogant attempt at some peculiar kind of other-worldliness, a rejection of ordinary experience. It begins in the humble recognition that human things can be very holy, full of God; whereas high-minded speculations about His nature need not be holy at all. Since all life is engulfed in Him, He can reach out to us anywhere and at any level. The depth and richness of His Eternal Being are unknown to us. Yet Christianity declares that this unsearchable Life, which is in essence a self-giving Love, and is wholly present wherever it loves, so loved this world as to desire to reveal within it the deepest secret of His thought; appearing within and through His small, fugitive, imperfect creatures, in closest union with humanity. In the beginning was the Word: and the Word was God, and without Him was not anything made that hath been made: and the Word became flesh and dwelt among us.

That seems immense. A complete philosophy is contained in it. And then we come down to the actual setting of this supreme event, and at once all our notions of the suitable and the significant are set aside; all our pet values reversed. A Baby, just that; and moreover, a Baby born in the most unfortunate circumstances. The extremes of the transcendent and the homely are suddenly brought together in this disconcerting revelation of reality. The hard life of the poor, its ceaseless preoccupation with the lowliest of human needs and duties, the absolute surrender and helplessness, the half-animal status of babyhood; all this is the chosen vehicle for the unmeasured inpouring of the Divine Life and Love. So too the strange simplicity of its beginning both rebukes and reassures us. It is like a quiet voice speaking in our deepest prayer: "The Lord is with thee . . ." and calling forth the one and only answer, "Behold the handmaid of the Lord, be it unto me according to thy Word!" Humble self-abandonment is found and declared to be enough to give us God. First in one way and then in another, all the incidents which cluster round the mystery of the Incarnation seem designed to show us this; the simplest yet the deepest truth about His relation to the soul.

For meditation: Human things can be very holy.

For prayer: Not under a Christmas tree nor in neatly wrapped packages, but in a bare barn visited by farmers you came once, Holy One, and where the need is greatest, you come now; guide me, gracious God, to seek you and serve you there and so to simplify my life that you will come also to me.

DECEMBER 31

Life Goes On

And now we turn from the central mystery to the clustered events, through which its character is disclosed. We see the new life growing in secret. Nothing very startling happens. We see the child in the carpenter's workshop. He does not go outside the frame of the homely life in which He appeared. It did quite well for Him, and will do quite well for us. . . . It is like the hidden life at Nazareth. We must be content with the wholesome routine of the nursery, doing ordinary things, learning ordinary lessons and eating ordinary food, if we are to grow truly and organically in wisdom and stature and favour with God and man. Growth in God is a far more gradual, less conscious process than we realize at first. We are so raw and superficial in our notions, that we cannot conceive the nature of those tremendous changes by which the child of grace becomes the man of God. We all want to be up and doing long before we are ready to do.

To contemplate the proportions of Christ's life is a terrible rebuke to spiritual impatience and uppish hurry. There we see how slow, according to our time-span, is the maturing of the thought of God. Ephemeral insects become adult in a few minutes, the new-born lamb gets up and starts grazing straight away, but the child depends for months on its mother's love. Sanctity, which is childhood in God, partakes of the long divine duration. We often feel that we ought to get on quickly, reach a new stage of knowledge or prayer, like spiritual may-flies. But Christ's short earthly life is divided into thirty years for growth and two and a half for action. The pause, the hush, the hiddenness, which intervenes between the Birth and the Ministry, is part of the divine method, and an earnest of the greatness of that which is to come. Only when that quiet growth has reached the right stage is there a revelation of God's purpose, and the stress and discipline of a crucial choice. Baptism, Fasting and Temptation come together as signs of maturity. It is much the same with us in the life of prayer. The Spirit fills us as we grow and make room. It keeps pace with us; does not suddenly stretch us like a pneumatic tyre, with dangerous results. To contemplate the life of Christ, said St. Augustine, "cures inflation, and nourishes humility." We see in Him the gradual action of God, subdued to the material on which it works, and fostering and sanctifying growth—that holy secret process—especially growth in the hidden, interior life, which is the unique source of His power in us.

For meditation: Growth in God is a far more gradual . . . process than we realize at first.

For prayer: Slow me down, Eternal God, and give me the gift of patience; teach me to treasure the gift of time and to let your grace work within me in your time frame, not mine.

January 1—Holy Name

Born for a Purpose

Beholding His Glory is only half our job. In our souls too the mysteries must be brought forth; we are not really Christians till that has been done. "The Eternal Birth," says Eckhart, "must take place in *you*." And another mystic says human nature is like a stable inhabited by the ox of passion and the ass of prejudice; animals which take up a lot of room and which I suppose most of us are feeding on the quiet. And it is there between them, pushing them out, that Christ must be born and in their very manger He must be laid—and they will be the first to fall on their knees before Him. Sometimes Christians seem far nearer to those animals than to Christ in His simple poverty, self-abandoned to God.

The birth of Christ in our souls is for a purpose beyond ourselves: it is because His manifestation in the world must be through us. Every Christian is, as it were, part of the dust-laden air which shall radiate the glowing Epiphany of God, catch and reflect His golden Light. *Ye are the light of the world*—but only because you are enkindled, made radiant by the One Light of the World. And being kindled, we have got to get on with it, be useful. As Christ said in one of His ironical flashes, "Do not light a candle in order to stick it under the bed!" Some people make a virtue of religious skulking.

For meditation: Christ must be made known through us.

For prayer: In a world of noise, Lord, how can my voice be heard? In a world of light, how can your glory be seen?

JANUARY 2

Shepherds and Magi

The Christmas Mystery has two parts: the Nativity and the Epiphany. A deep instinct made the Church separate these two feasts. In the first we commemorate God's humble entrance into human life, the emergence and birth of the Holy, and in the second its manifestation to the world, the revelation of the Supernatural made in that life. And the two phases concern our inner lives very closely too. The first only happens in order that the second may happen, and the second cannot happen without the first. Christ is a Light to lighten the Gentiles as well as the Glory of His people Israel. Think of what the Gentile was when these words were written—an absolute outsider. All cosy religious exclusiveness falls before that thought. The Light of the world is not the sanctuary lamp in your favourite church. It is easy for the devout to join up with the Shepherds and fall into place at the Crib and look out into the surrounding night and say, "Look at those extraordinary intellectuals wandering about after a star, with no religious sense at all! Look at that clumsy camel, what an unspiritual animal it is! We know the ox and the ass are the right animals to have! Look what queer gifts and odd types of self-consecration they are bringing; not the sort of people who come to church!" But remember that the Child who began by receiving these very unexpected pilgrims had a woman of the streets for His faithful friend and two thieves for His comrades at the end; and looking at these two extremes let us try to learn a little of the height and breadth and depth of His Love—and then apply it to our own lives.

It was said of Father Wainwright that he cared above all for scamps and drunkards and unbelievers—least for those who came regularly to church—and no man of our time was fuller of the Spirit of Christ. The first point about Epiphany is that *all* are called and welcomed and accepted. Our own loving adoration and deep certitude, if God in His mercy gives us that, is never to break our brotherhood with those who come longer journeys by other paths, led by a different star. The Magi took more trouble than the Shepherds. The intellectual virtues and intellectual longings of men are all blessed in Christ.

For meditation: *All* are called and welcomed and accepted.

For prayer: The Magi came from far away following a star that others failed to see; I have not always followed the short and straight route myself; grant that all who seek your light may find it; let me never be unbecoming to those who come.

JANUARY 3

The Magi

Now to accept historical Christianity as God's supreme self-revelation does not mean some elaborate philosophy of the spirit. It means accepting the Gospel story as touching our lives significantly at every point, because it is conveying God. If we are ever to learn all that this record can mean for us, we must never forget that these, beyond all other facts of history, are indwelt, moulded, brought into being by the Living Spirit of God, while plastic to His creative Thought. And if we thus feel God within these events, some so strange and some so homely, inspiring this action and record, then we also accept all these incidents as conveying something of His overruling Will and Thought, having something in them for each of us. Nothing is there by accident. Everything is there because it conveys spiritual truth, gives us the supernatural. It all "speaks to our condition" as Fox would say. The Synoptic Gospels may not always have the accuracy of a photograph but they have a higher reality, they are charged with God. That is the reason why meditation on the Gospels, chewing the evangelical cud, is so nourishing to the soul and so inexhaustible as a basis of prayer. In that sense every word of the Gospel is sacramental; and like some great work of art gives us more and more light and food, revealing greater depths of significance as we grow in the wisdom which is the child of humility and love. The Magi came away from Bethlehem much wiser than they were before.

For meditation: Every word of the Gospel is sacramental.

For prayer: Word by word, Word of God, let the Scripture speak to me with ever new and deeper meaning and guide us, like the Magi, to the place where I may kneel before you.

January 4

The Magi and Prayer

Look . . . at the story of the Magi: those scholars of the ancient world, turning from their abstruse calculations and searching of the heavens because they saw a new star, and driven to seek along fresh paths for a clue to the mystery of life. What they found does not seem at first sight what we should now call "intellectually satisfying." It was not a revelation of the Cosmic Mind, but a poor little family party; yet there they were brought to their knees—because, like the truly wise, they were really humble-minded—before a little, living, growing thing. The utmost man can achieve on his own here capitulates before the unspeakable and mysterious simplicity of the method of God; His stooping down to us. His self-disclosure at the very heart of life. After all, the shepherds got there long before the Magi; and even so, the animals were already in position when the shepherds arrived. He comes to His own; the God of our natural life makes of that natural life the very material of His self-revelation. His smile kindles the whole universe; His hallowing touch lies upon all life. The animal world and the natural world have their own rights and their own place within the Thought of God. There never was a religion more deeply in touch with natural things than Christianity, although it is infinite in its scope.

The essence of the story of the Magi is that it is no use to be too clever about life. Only in so far as we find God in it, do we find any meaning in it. Without Him it is a tissue of fugitive and untrustworthy pleasures, desires, conflicts, frustrations and intolerable pains. Historical Christianity need not involve for us an elaborate philosophy of the Spirit: but it does mean accepting as deeply significant all the great events of the Gospel, because conveying God. And, if we thus recognize the supernatural within these events, some so strange and some so homely; then, we also accept all these incidents as carrying a sacramental reference, conveying something of the over-ruling will and thought of God, and having something in them for each of us. If we are ever to learn all that this record can mean for us, we must never forget that these beyond all other facts of history, are indwelt and moulded by the Divine Charity.

For meditation: The Gospel is inexhaustible as a basis of prayer.

For prayer: Draw us, Holy One, as you drew the Magi, to those places and experiences in which we have not known you before, and open our eyes to see you and respond to you in love and awe and worship.

JANUARY 5

Light of the World

You know how sometimes on a pitch black night in the country, you see far off one glimmer of light and you follow it and it turns out to be just a candle in a cottage window—but it was enough to assure you of life ahead, to give you the lead you wanted in the dark. In the same way, when the Magi turned from their abstruse calculations in search of heaven and followed a star, they did not arrive at a great mathematical result or revelation of the cosmic mind. They found a poor little family party and were brought to their knees—because, like the truly wise, they were really humble-minded—before a baby born under most unfortunate circumstances, a mystery of human life, a little living growing thing. What a paradox! the apparently rich Magi coming to the apparently poor child. There they laid down their intellectual treasures—all pure gold to them—and, better than that, offered the spirit of adoration, the incense which alone consecrates the intellectual life and quest of truth, and that reverent acceptance of pain, mental suffering and sacrifice, that death to self which, like myrrh, hallows the dedicated life in all *its* forms.

The utmost man can achieve on his own here capitulates before the unspeakable simplicity of the methods of God. He is the Light of the World—all of it. He does not only want or illuminate spiritual things. His hallowing touch is for the ox and the ass, as afterwards for the sparrows and the flowers. There never was a less high-brow religion or one more deeply in touch with natural life than Christianity, although it is infinite in its scope. Whosoever shall humble himself as this little child, the same shall be greatest in the Kingdom of Heaven.

It is no use being too clever about life. Only so far as we find God in it do we find any meaning in it. Without Him it is a tissue of fugitive and untrustworthy pleasures, conflicts, ambitions, desires, frustrations, intolerable pain.

For meditation: It is no use being too clever about life.

For prayer: Light of the world, be my guide, show me where to go, show me where you are, show me the path of life.

January 6—The Epiphany

The Magi and New Birth

The story of the Magi shows the new life which has appeared within the rich texture of our normal experience, casting its purifying radiance upon the whole existence of manthe Light of the world, not the sanctuary lamp of a well-appointed church. Cosy religious exclusiveness is condemned in this mystery. It is easy for the pious to join the shepherds, and feel in place at the Crib, and look out into the surrounding darkness saying, "Look at those extraordinary intellectuals wandering about after a star; they seem to have no religious sense. Look what curious gifts and odd types of self-consecration they are bringing; not at all the sort of people one sees in church." Yet the child who began by receiving those unexpected pilgrims had a woman of the streets for His most faithful friend, and two thieves for His comrades at the last. Looking at these extremes, so deeply significant of the Christian spirit, we can learn something, perhaps, of the height and depth and breadth of that divine generosity into which our narrow and fragmentary loves must be absorbed. The Epiphany means the free pouring out of a limitless light—the Light of the World—not its careful communication to those whom we hold worthy to receive it. The Magi, after all, took more trouble than the shepherds. They came a longer journey, by more perilous paths. The intellectual virtues and longings of men are all blessed in Christ, "the intellectual radiance full of love."

We turn to another point which every mystery in its turn will show us; for they are there to light up the cycle of our own interior growth. And here again, God's mysterious and life-giving action in the soul is for a purpose that points beyond ourselves. It happens not merely for our sakes; but because His manifestation to the world must be through us. Every real Christian is part of the dust-laden air which shall radiate the glowing Charity of God; catch and reflect His golden light. Ye are the light of the world, because you are irradiated by the one Light of the World, the holy generosity of God. The great New Testament saints—in fact, all saints—look right through and past the outward appearance of men's lives, and seek only for the seed of the divine life within them, the hidden Child of God. "Ye are of God, little children," exclaims St. John "greater is He that is in you than he that is in the world." That is the awful truth which rules the inner life of man.

For meditation: Epiphany is the free pouring out of a limitless light.

For prayer: If indeed I am to radiate your light to the world, Lord Christ, then let that light burn within me to purge and purify until I know only you and seek only you and, finding you in everyone I meet, enable them to find you even in me.

References

November 27: *The Fruits of the Spirit*. Harrisburg, PA: Morehouse Publishing, 1982, 48–50.

November 28: Ibid., 50–52.

November 29: *The School of Charity*. London: Longmans, Green, and Co., 1954, 1–2.

November 30: Ibid., 6.

December 1: *The Fruits of the Spirit*, 5–7.

December 2: *Light of Christ*. Eugene, OR: Wipf and Stock Publishers, 50–51.

December 3: *The Fruits of the Spirit*, 43–45.

December 4: *The Life of the Spirit and the Life of Today*. Harrisburg, PA: Morehouse Publishing, 1994, 93.

December 5: *The Spiritual Life*. Harrisburg, PA: Morehouse Publishing, 1996, 14–17.

December 6: Ibid., 121–24.

December 7: Ibid., 78–81.

December 8: *The School of Charity*, 18–19.

December 9: *The Spiritual Life*, 73–76.

December 10: Ibid., 33–35.

December 11: Ibid., 109–11.

December 12: *Light of Christ*, 92–93.

December 13: Ibid., 72–73.

December 14: *Mystics of the Church*. Harrisburg, PA: Morehouse Publishing, 1988, 18–20.

December 15: *The Life of the Spirit and the Life of Today*, 158–59.
December 16: *The School of Charity*, 7–8.
December 17: *The Spiritual Life*, 55–58.
December 18: Ibid., 19–22.
December 19: *The School of Charity*, 16–18.
December 20: Ibid., 6–9.
December 21: *Light of Christ*, 27–28.
December 22: *The School of Charity*, 13–15.
December 23: *The Life of the Spirit and the Life of Today*, 156–58.
December 24: *The School of Charity*, 11, 13.
December 25: *Light of Christ*, 36–37.
December 26: *The School of Charity*, 39–40.
December 27: Ibid., 48–49.
December 28: *Light of Christ*, 45–46.
December 29: *The School of Charity*, 31–32.
December 30: Ibid., 40–41.
December 31: Ibid., 45–48.
January 1: *Light of Christ*, 41–42.
January 2: Ibid., 40–41.
January 3: Ibid., 39–40.
January 4: *The School of Charity*, 42–43.
January 5: *Light of Christ*, 37–39.
January 6: *The School of Charity*, 44–45.